Caribbean Primary Mathematics

Level 5 Teacher's Guide

Contents

Introduction

The *Caribbean Primary Mathematics* series was originally developed and tested by members of the UWI School of Education and schools. This new edition has been revised by a pan-Caribbean team of educational experts, with the following features.

Up-to-date curriculum objectives

We have updated the tried and tested course to meet the requirements of the latest curriculum in each of the Caribbean territories. In each Teacher's Guide, you will find a grid that outlines how the curriculum objectives are covered in the course for that level. In some cases, a concept may not be required by the curriculum of all the territories. You will find notes in the suggested approach for each chapter pointing out which activities to leave out if they are not relevant to your students.

Spiralling within each chapter

In Levels 4, 5 and 6, the series continues to follow the spiral approach to learning. Spiralling means that every new concept is reinforced at calculated levels and extended as time goes on. However, from Level 4 upwards, the material is divided into chapters. This helps students to deal cohesively with each concept, and also helps them to make the transition from hands-on Pupil Books to textbooks.

Relevant contexts for learning

Throughout each level, you will find 'talk about' boxes, illustrated with the CPM parrot, which provide topics for class discussions around topical issues relevant to the material covered on that page.

Interactive CD-Rom activities

In the new edition of *Caribbean Primary Mathematics*, each level comes with a CD-Rom packed with interactive activities for students to consolidate their learning of the key topics. There are references throughout the Teacher's Guide indicating when these activities are to be played. These are marked with the symbol .

Practical activities

Wherever you see the in the Pupil Book, students have an opportunity to explore or investigate a mathematical concept through a practical, hands-on activity. If you need any resources for these activities, they will be listed under materials at the beginning of the suggested approach for that chapter.

Classroom testing and additional activities

In the Pupil's Book, assessment material is provided at the end of each cluster of chapters dealing with related mathematical concepts. In the Teacher's Guide, we provide additional assessment material for some chapters, giving you the opportunity to assess your students' progress and identify areas that require more practice. We also provide many additional activities.

Approaches to computation

You need to make the students aware that some situations require the use of calculators, while others require a combination of mental or pencil and paper working. Students need to learn when to use the most appropriate strategy in a given situation.

When students come across a problem that they cannot easily work out mentally, they should get into the habit of first estimating the answer. This will help them to know if they have carried out the calculation correctly or not. Students should also check the reasonableness of their answers. This is especially important in word problems. Students should look back at the question and decide whether they have answered the question that was being asked and if their answer makes sense in the context of the problem.

Lesson planning

It is important that you plan your lessons before entering the classroom. Whether the plan is very detailed or only a brief outline of the activities to be carried out, it helps you to keep a record of what is to be taught. A lesson plan describes what is to be done, when it is to be done, how long it should take and what resources are needed.

One form of the lesson plan that is used widely in mathematics is known as the *Hunter Lesson Cycle*, so named because of the way the sequence of events may be repeated. The components of the Hunter Lesson Cycle are:
1 Set the stage.
2 State the objective.
3 Provide instructional input.
4 Model operations.
5 Check for understanding.
6 Give guided practice.
7 Give independent practice.

You may want to follow the Hunter Lesson Cycle, or you could use a more informal plan. Any lesson plan has three main components: the beginning, the middle and the end.

Beginning
- Set out the purpose of the lesson.
- Make connections to previous lessons or material covered.
- Initiate a participatory activity which stimulates the students' interest in the lesson.

Middle
- Introduce the mathematical concepts.
- Demonstrate some examples of what the students are expected to do.
- Give students time to complete their activities and tasks.
- Assess and evaluate the students' work.

End

- Summarise the lesson and learning activities, orally or through an activity.
- Indicate what the follow-up to the lesson will be.

Assessment

Traditionally, assessment has comprised mainly written tests. While these are important in determining the progress of students, especially when a grade or mark is required, there are other forms of assessment that should be included in the mathematics classroom:

- questions and tasks
- practical investigations and activities
- homework
- group work
- self assessment.

Questions and tasks

Remember, you cannot assess all students at the same time. During any lesson, ask questions and set tasks that allow you to assess some of the students. Gradually, you will build up a clear idea of each student's progress. Make sure that the questions are clear and that students know what they are expected to do.

Practical investigations and activities

Most practical activities require pair work or group work. The students will often have to share their answers with the rest of the class. This provides an opportunity for you to assess problem solving and presentation skills. Some investigations can be completed as homework.

Group work

Group work gives you an opportunity to assess each student's social and communication skills. More confident students will often dominate the group; make sure that you ask questions aimed at the shyer members of the group in order to assess their contributions too.

Self assessment

In many cases, you can ask students to check each other's work or their own work. It is also important to ask students which parts of the lesson they found easiest or most difficult, as they often have a clear idea of the areas in which they want more practice.

Assess readiness

↓

Set the stage
- Motivate

↓

State the objective
- Relate to prior knowledge

▶

Provide instructional input
- Label concepts
- Define terms and symbols

▼

Model operations

◀

Check for understanding
- Ask questions
- Observe operations
- Reteach, if necessary

▼

Give guided practice
- Students demonstrate skills
- Students extend concepts
- Students work examples
- Students repeat operations

▼

Give independent practice
- Students practise skills

▼

Assess mastery
- Ask questions
- Observe students
- Give tests

Integration

Integration should be included in all aspects of mathematics instruction, both within mathematics and across mathematics and other subject areas. Firstly, within mathematics, a topic such as money cannot be introduced or reviewed without reference to related topics such as decimals, operations on numbers and place value. Secondly, many topics in mathematics are common to topics in other subject areas; measurement in Science, shapes in Art and map locations in Social Studies can all be reinforced in the mathematics classroom. Integration provides opportunities for you to plan more effective lessons, in collaboration with other subject teachers. This helps the students to recognise that mathematics is not an isolated subject but a component of all other subjects.

Technology

Technology should form an integral part of all mathematics instruction for use by both the teacher and the student. This may include computers, overhead projectors, televisions, tape recorders and, of course, calculators. Computers provide immediate access to worldwide resources, visual stimuli and simulations of otherwise remote activities, and contact with learners in other places. In addition to these benefits, there are many other advantages to using technology in schools. Technology enhances the motivation of the learner in many ways. Students see technology as something fun and exciting. It immediately grabs their attention. Technology also enhances creativity as students have the opportunity to create their own materials. Each student can determine the pace at which to proceed and thus gains more control over the learning that takes place. Technology helps you to produce resources and assignments, to execute varied and interesting lessons and to store these materials efficiently over long periods. Technology is therefore an asset for both you and the student.

Problem solving

Although problem solving is an integral part of mathematics instruction, many teachers teach problem solving as a separate concept. Instead, problem solving should be incorporated at all stages of the instructional process – when introducing a concept, throughout the instruction and as part of the assessment. Problem solving provides an opportunity for students to communicate in the mathematics classroom, reason, explore and investigate, while grasping a better understanding of the concepts.

There are four general stages in finding the solution to a problem. These stages are:
- understanding the problem
- devising a plan
- carrying out the plan
- checking the solution.

There are many problem-solving strategies that may be used, depending on the problem to be solved. These include:
- drawing a diagram
- guessing and checking/trial and error
- solving a simpler problem
- acting out the problem
- making a model
- looking for a pattern.

Realistic and practical activities

Mathematics must be taught in such a way that the students enjoy what they are doing and relate it to their everyday lives. In addition to the activities suggested in the *Caribbean Primary Mathematics* series, you should ensure that their lessons include activities that are realistic and practical. In addition, the students must recognise the link between mathematics and their daily lives and experiences. We all use mathematics on a daily basis: we tell the time, we measure amounts when we serve and eat food, we estimate whether clothing will fit, we read maps ... just to name a few daily mathematical processes. Carpenters, painters, accountants and doctors are some of the people who depend on a knowledge of mathematics daily. For children, activities such as running races, skipping and playing card games all involve some mathematical understanding. These types of activities are ideal for teaching mathematics to ensure that all children, especially those who struggle with mathematics, become more confident and competent in their mathematical abilities.

Teaching and learning materials

Learning aids enable students to develop their mathematical knowledge and competencies. Pupil books and textbooks are examples of everyday learning aids. However, in order for students to gain real understanding of mathematics, they need to encounter a range of teaching and learning materials that give them practical experience in using mathematical concepts. This chapter tells you about the range of materials that you can use in your classroom. We offer suggestions about obtaining and using mathematics materials. The chapter presents detailed information about:

- the importance of mathematics materials
- types of materials
- how to build up a collection of materials
- how to use different types of materials in your classroom
- activities related to specific materials.

At the end of the chapter, you will also find some photocopiable materials which you can copy for use in your classroom.

The importance of teaching and learning materials

Teaching and learning materials are important because they:
- engage the students in practical, hands-on learning
- offer concrete examples and applications of mathematical concepts, skills and procedures
- stimulate interest, perseverance and problem-solving skills.

Each of these points is discussed in more detail below.

Combining hands-on activity with mental activity

Students learn best by doing things and being actively engaged in the teaching/learning process. Active engagement may involve physical activity, but it should always require some form of mental activity (Anthony, 1996). For example, students may examine or use selected objects. While doing this, the students should also be required to engage in mental activities such as justifying, discussing, comparing and contrasting mathematical ideas. Learning materials facilitate practical activities which also engage students mentally.

Progressing from the concrete to the abstract

Students at the primary level are seldom able to do mathematics only at the symbolic or abstract level. Teaching and learning materials enable students to examine specific examples of concepts, skills and procedures and to generalise from these examples. The materials also allow students to link the mathematical concepts to their experiences and to previous learning. Thus teaching and learning materials can help students to learn mathematics meaningfully.

Stimulating students' interest and perseverance

Well-prepared, appropriate materials capture the students' attention, motivating them to engage with the mathematical learning process and stimulating their interest in mathematical tasks. In this way, teaching and learning materials develop students' problem-solving skills. Personal qualities – such as perseverance and willingness to engage in tasks – facilitate mathematical learning, but these qualities are also improved through the use of mathematical learning and teaching materials.

Types of materials

You can use a wide range of materials in your classroom, including found objects and materials, second-hand items and bought products. In this section we categorise materials in two different ways:
- according to the stages of mathematical development supported by each material
- according to the form of the material.

There are many other ways of categorising materials, but this section aims to give you a broad idea of the variety of materials available.

Supporting mathematical development through materials

In this course, we recommend that students begin with concrete examples and gradually move towards working with abstract concepts. Grossnickle, Reckzeh, Perry and Ganoe (1983) divide materials into three groups, which are linked with this progression from concrete to abstract:
- **Manipulatives** are concrete objects that the students can feel, touch, handle and move. Examples include dice, cards, paper, clay and string. These materials are linked to the concrete stage of mathematical development.
- **Visual, audio and audio-visual materials** require students to use their senses of sight and hearing. Visual materials require the student to engage by looking or watching. Examples include pictures, diagrams and photographs. Audio materials involve hearing or listening. Examples include CDs, cassette tapes, rhymes and songs. Audio-visual materials involve a combination of watching and listening. Examples include films, videos and some computer software. These materials are linked to a semi-concrete stage of mathematical development.
- **Symbolic materials** represent mathematics through words, numbers and symbols. Examples include textbooks, pupil books, worksheets and other texts. Symbolic materials are linked to the abstract stage of mathematical development.

In order to progress from the concrete to the abstract when teaching each mathematical skill or concept, you would usually introduce the work using manipulatives. You could then gradually move towards using audio-visual materials, and finally progress towards using symbolic materials.

Different forms of materials

We can also categorise materials according to form. Here, materials take four different forms: manipulatives, print materials, games and puzzles, and technological devices. The table below outlines these forms and gives some examples of each. Remember, these categories are not mutually exclusive. For example, software packages could include games and puzzles as well as print media. However, this table is intended to give you an idea of the sheer range of materials available.

Type of material	Description	Examples
Manipulatives	Materials that students can handle, feel, touch and move	■ Real-life objects such as shells, seeds, buttons, money ■ Objects specifically designed to represent mathematical ideas, e.g. geo-boards, abaci, base ten blocks, geometrical shapes or models
Print materials	Materials that convey information in words, pictures or diagrams	■ Activity cards that outline tasks ■ Pupil books and worksheets ■ Flash cards ■ Charts
Games and puzzles	Games are activities that are guided by rules; puzzles are non-routine problems	■ Commercial games, e.g. snakes and ladders, dominoes, card games ■ Teacher- or student-made puzzles and games
Technological devices	Materials that require electronic or other technology	■ Calculators, films, videos, audio cassettes/CDs, computer software packages

Resources in and around your classroom

Immediate resources

Your classroom is an immediate source of learning materials. Many everyday objects can be used for measurement and data collection activities, and for developing number concepts and computation strategies. Examples include:
■ parts of the classroom – floor, door, windows, board, and so on
■ furniture – desks, chairs, cupboards, shelves, and so on
■ students' possessions – pencils, rulers, pens, school bags, lunch boxes, and so on.

The school compound beyond your classroom is also a rich source of materials. Students can explore mathematical concepts such as symmetry by examining the school buildings, playground, plants and trees. The activities that take place within the school compound also provide learning opportunities. For example, students could carry out investigations to determine the most popular games, sports, lunch foods, and so on. Each school compound is different, so you should explore your school compound to determine how it can be used to teach mathematics.

A classroom bulletin board

A classroom bulletin board allows you to display work and share ideas. To set up a bulletin board, you may designate an area of wall space or use a board made of soft wood such as chipboard. Work together with your students to prepare and monitor the bulletin board displays. In Levels 1 to 3, you will need to take responsibility for maintaining the display. From Level 4 upwards, the students can take on more responsibility for preparing and maintaining the display. Use the bulletin board to:

- pose problems and puzzles
- explain solutions to displayed problems and puzzles
- elicit examples of concepts
- display the results of data collection exercises
- display pictures and examples of how mathematics is used in real life (graphs, maps, and so on).

Your students may learn from the displays independently, in their own time. However, you should actively use the bulletin board by discussing the displays with the students and using the discussions for informal assessment purposes.

Learning centres

You can also set up a learning centre in your classroom. The learning centre is an area where you store enrichment activities and materials at varying levels of difficulty. Check and comment on students' work and provide guidance for possible follow-up activities.

Building up a collection of materials

Students are most likely to use materials that are readily available in the classroom. So it is a good idea to build up a varied collection of learning materials for your classroom.

Selecting appropriate materials

When selecting materials, ask yourself the following questions:

- Are the materials directly related to the concepts or skills being developed?
- Do the materials facilitate the students' movement from one level of abstraction to another, for example from the concrete to the abstract?
- Are the materials appropriate for the ages and developmental level of your students?
- Are the materials big/small enough for the students to use easily?
- Does the level of complexity of the materials match your students' mathematical development and needs?
- Are the materials challenging enough/easy enough?
- Will the materials stimulate the students' interest?

The following list gives you an idea of the types of materials that could be used in teaching the various content areas. Note that the list is not exhaustive and the assignment of materials to particular content areas is not definitive. Some materials are suitable for teaching a variety of content areas or topics, as necessary and when appropriate.

Content areas	Manipulative	Print materials	Games and puzzles	Technological devices
Number concepts and computation	Common objects, e.g. buttons, seeds, stones, sticks; base ten blocks; place value charts or pockets; hundred charts; sorting trays; attribute blocks; sand boxes; Cuisenaire rods; abaci (counting frames); fraction sets	Numeral and base facts; flash cards; stories with a mathematical theme; number lines	Numeral jigsaw puzzles; colour-by-number puzzles; dominoes	Calculators
Measurement	Ruler; measuring tapes; clocks; watches and watch faces; measuring cylinders; cups; spoons; thermometers; balance and scales; various containers; string, trundle and wheel	Simple maps; calendars; squared paper		
Money	Coins; notes; play money notes	Advertisements		Calculators
Geometry	Models of 2D and 3D shapes; geo-board; tangram pieces; drinking straws; string; attribute blocks	Dots and squared paper	Battleship game	
Statistics and data handling	Building blocks; dice	Newspaper and magazine clippings of graphs; squared paper		

Acquiring materials

The quickest way to acquire materials is to buy them. However, this can be unnecessarily expensive. There are many inexpensive, effective ways of building up a collection of learning materials. Here are some suggestions:

- Collect manipulatives such as shells, seeds, stones, sticks and beads.
- Prepare your own fraction pieces from sheets of card or plastic.
- Prepare place value charts using Bristol board.
- Involve parents in constructing materials such as geo-boards, sets of 3D shapes, abaci and so on.
- Involve students in constructing simple materials such as clock faces, tangram pieces, equivalent fraction charts, and so on.

If you decide to construct materials, first find a well-prepared commercial or local example of the material, note its mathematical properties and ensure that these properties are features of your constructed materials. For example, when guiding your students to construct equivalent fraction charts, ensure that the fractional parts have been divided correctly.

Whether you purchase or construct your materials, ensure that they are attractive, durable and safe to use. Protect re-usable materials from damage so that they can be used repeatedly. Laminate materials such as charts and work cards, and store all materials in a cool, dry place. You can use cardboard boxes or inexpensive plastic bins as containers.

Using materials in the mathematics classroom

You can use materials in your classroom in several ways. For example, you could use materials to:

- facilitate the use of teaching methods such as guided discovery and co-operative learning groups
- provide enrichment activities
- cater for students' individual abilities and allow them to progress at different rates
- introduce new concepts
- initiate investigations
- generate discussions.

As far as is possible and appropriate, the students themselves should work with the materials – either on their own or with your guidance – in order to explore mathematical ideas. When you use the materials for demonstration or instruction purposes, make sure that you select materials that are large enough for the students to see easily.

Several factors influence how effectively the teaching or learning materials enhance students' learning. Some of these factors are:

- the students' readiness for materials
- the quality of the materials
- the appropriateness of the materials for developing the mathematical ideas of the lesson.

Some general and specific guidelines for using materials in your classroom follow.

General guidelines

- Check your supplies. Ensure that you have sufficient materials so that each student can have the quantity of materials necessary to develop the intended concept, skill or procedure.
- Plan properly. Before the lesson, select the materials you want to use, and plan how to integrate them into the lesson. Sometimes, during the lesson, you may find that students need other materials; adjust your lesson and include the use of other materials as necessary.
- Get to know the material. Acquaint yourself with the materials before introducing them to your students. If you are unfamiliar with the materials, practise using them yourself before the lesson. Preview print material, films, videos and computer software in order to identify the mathematical concepts and vocabulary that students should have acquired in order to use the materials successfully.
- Use a range of materials. There are a variety of ways to teach each mathematical concept, skill or procedure. For example, when students are learning about place value, they could use abaci, ice-cream sticks, base ten blocks, place value charts, and so on. A variety of materials appeals to students' different interests and learning styles. Also, as students identify differences and similarities in the representations, they will gradually abstract the relevant mathematical ideas.
- Make sure students understand what to do with the materials. Let the students play with new or unfamiliar materials before you use them formally in a lesson. Ask questions to find out what they learned about the materials, and use these observations as a basis for the formal use of the materials in the classroom. Ensure that the students understand the purpose of using the materials and how to use them.
- Evaluate the use of the materials after each lesson. Ask yourself: Were the students motivated? Did they understand what to do with the materials? What difficulties, if any, arose during the lesson? Did the materials help the students to develop the intended learning outcomes?

Guidelines for using manipulatives

- Monitor your students' progress. Allow them to work with manipulatives until they are ready to move onto semi-concrete or symbolic representations. Also remember that if you let students continue working with manipulatives for too long, they may become bored and demotivated. Always monitor your students' progress to determine the most appropriate time for them to move on to other materials or activities.
- Ask questions. Encourage students to talk about what they are doing and understanding as they use manipulatives. Their comments may be used for assessment purposes and to guide the development of your lessons.

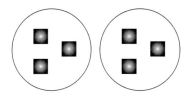

Guidelines for using print materials

- Encourage your students to describe pictures, drawings and diagrams. They should identify components such as lines, shapes, labels, and so on. Encourage them to interpret and discuss the meanings of each component. For example, students should be able to discuss the various ways they could interpret a diagram such as the one shown on the left.
- Use print materials such as textbooks, pupil books, newspaper clippings, and so on for a variety of purposes. For example, students may use these materials as a source of information, for drills and practice exercises, or for checking generalisations that they have developed.
- Use manipulatives to help students gain understanding of the mathematical ideas and vocabulary in the print material.
- Make sure that the language and instructions are clear, easy-to-use and pitched at the students' level of development. The mathematical language should always be used accurately, information should be well-spaced and easy-to-read, and pictures and diagrams should reinforce the ideas and make reading easier.

Guidelines for using games and puzzles

- Build up your collection of games and puzzles by encouraging students to develop their own games and puzzles. Develop new games by adapting the rules and actions of existing games.
- Each time you play a game, make sure students understand the rules.
- Monitor your students' progress during games. Check their use of mathematical concepts or skills required by the game. Note their strengths, weaknesses and misconceptions.
- During the game or puzzle session, discuss the students' responses with them. Encourage them to explain what they learned and to identify their difficulties. Follow up with appropriate activities to help them to improve.

Guidelines for using technological devices

- Prepare your students for using technological materials. Introduce the key ideas, concepts and vocabulary they will hear, see or use.
- Use follow-up activities to review, evaluate and reinforce the mathematical ideas used in the materials.

Using selected materials

Geo-boards

A geo-board is a piece of board with an array of pegs or nails securely fastened to the board. Although the sizes of geo-boards may vary, an appropriate size for students is a 20 cm × 20 cm board with five rows of five nails or pegs (for younger students) or ten rows of ten nails or pegs (for older students). They can stretch rubber bands around the nails or pegs to make different kinds of shapes.

Geo-boards may help students develop and consolidate geometrical concepts related to plane shapes, for example polygons, curves, lines and symmetry.

Activities

Ask students to make different types of shapes on their geo-boards and to describe them. For example:

- Make a four-sided figure. How many different four-sided figures can you make? Describe and name these shapes.
- Make a triangle with one right angle. Take another rubber band and make another triangle so that your first triangle changes to a rectangle. Explain what you did to make the rectangle.
- How many rectangles with an area of 24 cm² can you make on your geo-board? Write down the lengths of their sides.
- Make a quadrilateral whose area is the same as its perimeter. Describe your shape.

These types of activities could be followed up by activities involving drawing shapes on dotted, square, graph or plain paper.

Tangram puzzles

Tangram puzzles are made up of seven shapes cut from a square piece of paper, as shown here. Use heavy paper such as cardboard or Bristol board. If these are unavailable, use plain paper. You should provide younger students with the pieces; older students may make their own.

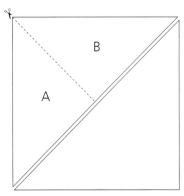

Instructions for making tangram pieces

- Start with a square piece of paper.
- Fold the square in half to make two triangles (A and B). Mark the fold line with a pencil or crayon. Cut along the fold line.
- Take one of the triangles and fold it in half to make two, smaller triangles. Cut along the fold. Set aside the two triangles.
- Take the other large triangle. Place the cut edge horizontally. Take the top point and fold it down until it touches the middle of the long cut edge. Open it again. The fold should make a small triangle at the top of the paper (C). Cut along the fold as shown in the picture. Then place this small triangle with your other two completed pieces.

- Place the remaining piece horizontally on your desk. Fold it in half and cut along the fold line as shown.
- Take one of the halves. Turn your paper so that the longest side is on the bottom. Place this side horizontally on your desk. Fold the longest side so that you get a square and a triangle (D and E). Cut along the fold line. Set aside these pieces with your other completed pieces.

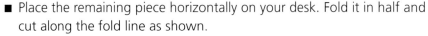

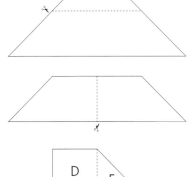

- Take the remaining piece and fold it so that the 90 degree angle touches the angle opposite it (F and G). Cut along the fold line.
- You should now have the seven pieces of the tangram puzzle.

Activities

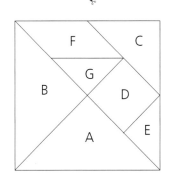

- Put the pieces back to form the original square.
- Name the shapes of the seven pieces.
- Make other geometrical shapes using a combination of the pieces. For example: make a triangle using two triangular pieces – E and G; make a square using three of the pieces – C, G and E; make a rectangle using four triangles and one quadrilateral – A, B, F, E and G.
- Make everyday shapes such as a boat, or a bird, using all or some of the pieces.

Worksheets

You may design worksheets in such a way that they are self-correcting. For example, you could have a puzzle in a worksheet. As the students attempt to solve the puzzle, they would get an indication as to whether their responses to the tasks are correct. If they solve the puzzle, their responses are most likely correct. The puzzle may take the form of words or phrases that the students have to complete. An example is given below.

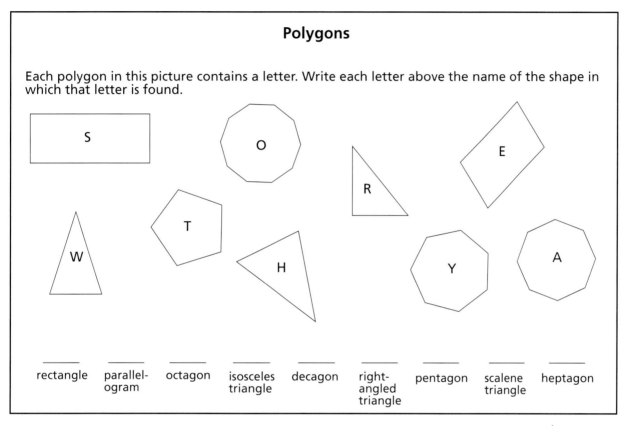

Polygons

Each polygon in this picture contains a letter. Write each letter above the name of the shape in which that letter is found.

rectangle	parallel-ogram	octagon	isosceles triangle	decagon	right-angled triangle	pentagon	scalene triangle	heptagon

Calculators

Use calculators for the following purposes:

- to investigate concepts and problems requiring computation strategies beyond the students' level
- to build up strategies for recalling basic facts
- to study real-life situations.

To help your students learn to use calculators sensibly, you should model the appropriate use of calculators in a variety of situations. You should also make them aware that some situations may require the use of calculators, while others may require a combination of mental or pencil-and-paper working; they should use the most appropriate strategy in a given situation.

Activities

Help your students to understand the functions of the calculator keys. For example, you could ask the students to press a key or a series of keys and note what happens on the display. Let them discuss whether their calculators operate in different ways.

You can use calculators with younger students to help them practise counting. Ask the students to key in 1 + = = = ... and to note what happens. Some calculators might require the following sequence for counting: 1 + + = = ... As the students progress to skip counting and counting backwards, let them speculate as to how their calculators will perform these functions. Then they should check the accuracy of their speculations.

Use calculator games to help develop students' reasoning skills. Two examples are outlined below.

■ Students can work in pairs. Each student keys in a number, for example 25, into his or her calculator. Each student then uses any combination of the four operations (+, − , × ,÷) to get an answer of 0. Multiplication by 0 and division by 0 are not allowed. The student who gets to 0 using the fewest operations is the winner.

■ Students work in pairs using one calculator per pair. They key in a number, for example 100. The first player subtracts any number from 1 to 9 (including 1 and 9). The second player does the same, this time subtracting from the difference that is on the display. The players alternate turns. If a player subtracts a number to get 0, that player loses the game.

Calculators allow students to explore calculations involving the four basic operations. The following are some related activities.

■ Let students use their calculators to multiply a set of numbers by 10, 100 and 1 000. Let them record their answers, then examine the results for any patterns that would provide a way of obtaining the answers without the calculator. This activity can be extended to multiplication and division of decimals.

■ Write a multiplication statement on the board, such as 5 × 13 × 7. Let the students use their calculators to find the answers. Multiply one of the factors in the statement above by 3, for example 5 × 13 × 21. Let the students find the answer using their calculators. Record the answer. Let them find the answers to the other two possible cases: 15 × 13 × 7 and 5 × 39 × 7. Repeat using other statements and multiplication by other numbers. Ask the class for its observations. Let students explain what would happen to the product of a set of numbers if any one number in the set were multiplied by another factor. Guide the students to explore how the product would be affected if every number in the set were multiplied by the same number in turn.

Photocopiable materials

The following are some materials that you can copy for use in your class.

Decimal paper

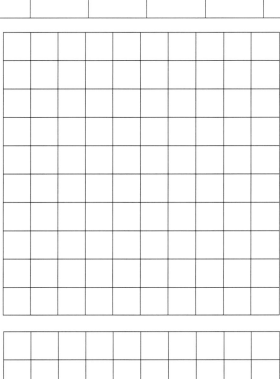

Fraction strips

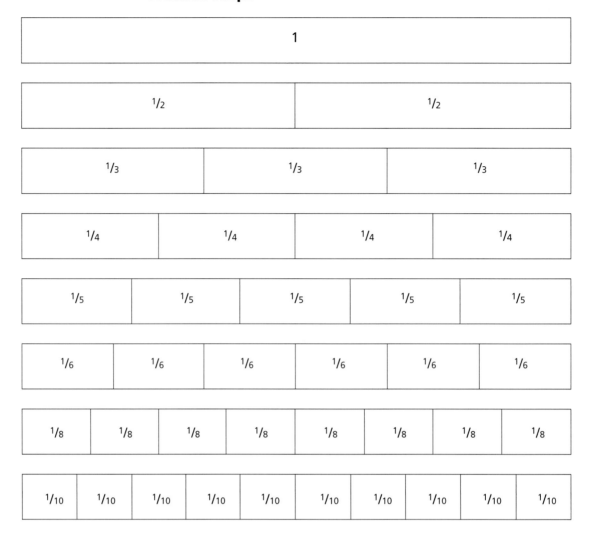

References and further reading

Anthony, G. (1996). 'Active learning in a constructivist framework', *Educational Studies in Mathematics*, 41 (3), 3–11.

Grossnickle, F.E., Reckzeh, J., Perry, L.M. & Ganoe, N.S. (1983). *Discovering meanings in elementary school mathematics* (7th ed.), New York: Holt, Rinehart & Winston.

Lemlech, J.K. (1998). *Curriculum and instructional methods for the elementary and middle school* (4th ed.), Upper Saddle River, NJ: Merrill.

Sheffield, L. & Cruikshank, D.E. (2000). *Teaching and learning elementary and middle school mathematics* (4th ed.), New York: John Wiley.

Chapter-by-chapter support

Chapter 1 Number theory

Pupil Book pages 5 to 10

Materials

- reference material such as encyclopaedias, history books and Internet access
- abacus
- place value charts
- number lines drawn on posters
- big jar filled with sweets for estimating
- flash cards with the basic Roman numerals
- clocks and watches that show Roman numerals

Objectives

Students should be able to:

- ✅ read, write and order numbers
- ✅ determine place value of a digit in a given number
- ✅ write numbers using expanded notation
- ✅ round numbers off to the nearest ten, 100 or 1 000
- ✅ read and write Roman numerals
- ✅ express Hindu–Arabic numbers as Roman numerals and vice versa.

Suggested approach

Please note that Jamaican students are required to work with up to eight-digit numbers, students in St Lucia are required to work with up to six-digit numbers, students in OECS territories are required to work with up to five-digit numbers, and students in Trinidad are required to work with up to seven-digit numbers. Teachers in each area should provide examples within the appropriate number range for their students.

Review place value with students, using an abacus or similar device. Ensure that they understand that the same digit written in a different position or place will have a different value. Complete examples such as:

- Determine the value of the digit 5 in the numbers below. Write the answers in words.

  215   354   528   15 678

Using a place value chart, show students how to determine the number names, moving from single digits and progressing through tens, hundreds, etc. Students should be able to write the number names for the numbers 1 to 100, before writing the number names for 100 to 900. Finally, they can progress to the number names for thousands. Ensure that students use the place values to assist in writing the number names. Use the place value chart to show how the numbers can be expressed in expanded form. Then the students can work through the exercises on pages 5 and 6 and exercise 2 at the top of page 7.

In the counting section on page 7, students revise counting on, counting backwards and skip counting. They have come across all these terms in the previous levels. Go through the example with the students. Emphasise the need to find the direction and the interval each time.

Go through some more examples of your own on the board. Use a number line at first if you think it is necessary. For each example, ask the students the direction and the interval in which they have to count. Students can then complete the exercises on page 7.

Next, move on to ordering numbers. First, teach the students to order numbers with the same number of digits, for example: 271, 258, 219. Give a few examples for the class to work through.

With numbers of different sizes, a good strategy is to arrange them in groups with the same number of digits and order within the smaller groups. Below is a worked example.
- Write the following numbers in order, starting with the smallest: 659, 2 358, 1 128, 18 913, 1 435, 581, 36, 13 264, 634, 43, 920.

The first groupings will look like this:

43	659	2 358	18 913
36	581	1 128	13 264
	634	1 435	
	920		

The first ordering within groups will look like this:

36	581	1 128	13 264
43	634	1 435	18 913
	659	2 358	
	920		

The final order can then be written as follows: 36, 43, 581, 634, 659, 920, 1 128, 1 435, 2 358, 13 264, 18 913.

The 'talk about' box on page 8 asks students to think about why it is sometimes useful to order numbers by size. There are many different contexts in which we use ordering. For example, sometimes we order items in order of size (for example, clothing, different lengths of materials such as fabric, wood or paper). When people vote, the ballots are counted so that the parties that received the most votes will win the election. Students may think of many other examples. Have them work through the exercises on page 8 in order to practise ordering numbers.

Introduce the concept of rounding off by asking questions such as:
- How many children are in the school – is the number close to 100, 200, 300 or 400?
- How many people can fit into a bus?
- How many books do you think there are on the bookshelf?
- How many sweets are in this jar?

Chapter-by-chapter support

The students can give their answers. Select the nearest-to-correct answer. Discuss how we identify the most suitable answer. Introduce the idea of an estimate of a true value. Work through Section A on page 9 with the class. Write the list below on the board, and ask the students to identify which of the measurements could be given as an estimate and which should be accurate; they can tick the items which should be accurate.

Should we estimate or measure accurately:
- the number of persons at a concert
- the price of a ticket to a concert
- the cost of a bicycle
- the height of a student
- the height of a bridge
- the pounds of flour needed to bake a cake
- the number of trees in a park?

Discuss with the students situations where an estimate could be used and situations where the use of an estimate may cause a problem.

Draw a number line on the board, from 0 to 40, as shown.

```
0     5     10    15    20    25    30    35    40
|ₗₗₗₗ|ₗₗₗₗ|ₗₗₗₗ|ₗₗₗₗ|ₗₗₗₗ|ₗₗₗₗ|ₗₗₗₗ|ₗₗₗₗ|
```

Use a number line to show how numbers such as 21, 23, 26, 34, 38 are rounded off to the nearest ten. (You may want to prepare the number line on a poster, or you could draw it on the board.) Emphasise that numbers with five or more ones get rounded up to the next ten; numbers with four or fewer ones get rounded down to the last ten. Use a number line with hundreds to show how to round off numbers such as 136, 158, 151, 148 and so on. When rounding off hundreds, we look at the tens place – if the number has five or more tens, we round it up to the next hundred, and so on. Have the students work through further examples on the board. Then they can work through Section B on page 9. Go through their answers with them.

CD-Rom activity
- Rounding off numbers

CD-Rom activity
- Roman numerals

Turn to page 10. Read through the information at the top of the page. Give a brief history of Roman numerals, pointing out that these numerals were used by the Romans for almost 2 000 years. Go through the Roman numerals again, using the flash cards. Then show the students how to write some basic Roman numerals, for example 1, 5 and 10. Do quite a few examples with the students. Then students can work through Pupil Book page 10. They should answer the 'talk about' box as part of their written exercise.

Additional activities
Number theory is an area with many opportunities for integration. Some examples are given below.

Building up and breaking down numbers
You can make a place value chart. You will need ten strips of card of equal length for each place value. For ones, use ten strips that are 3 cm long each; for tens, use ten strips that are 6 cm long each; for hundreds, use ten strips that are 9 cm long each; for thousands, use ten strips that are 12 cm long each. Place the digits 1 to 9 on the ones cards, the numbers 10, 20, 30 to 90 on the tens cards and the numbers 100, 200, 300 to 900 on the hundreds cards, and so on. The idea is to build up or break down numbers by putting a set of cards on top of each other. For example, to show the number 3 568, we would need a card that shows 3 000, one that shows 500, one that shows 60 and one that shows 8.

Different counting systems
Research early civilisations (for example Egyptian, Hebrew and Mayan counting systems). Find out which symbols these peoples used to represent numbers.

Population density
Population density is the number of people per square mile/kilometre in an area. Discuss this topic, and use research resources (such as books, the Internet, and so on) to research the population density of various countries. Also discuss some of the issues raised by overpopulation – the availability of enough food and water, traffic problems, housing shortages, and so on.

Chapter 2   Factors and multiples

Pupil Book pages 11 to 15

Materials
- charts giving definitions of multiples and factors with examples
- chart showing an example of a factor tree

Objectives
Students should be able to:
- ✓ identify and use the factors of a given number
- ✓ identify and use prime numbers
- ✓ distinguish between prime and composite numbers
- ✓ express a number as a product of its prime factors
- ✓ determine the highest common factor (HCF) of two numbers
- ✓ identify and use the multiples of a given number
- ✓ determine the lowest common multiple (LCM) of two or three numbers
- ✓ classify numbers using several number concepts, e.g. prime and even, prime and odd, composite and odd, etc
- ✓ complete number sequences.

Suggested approach

Review the term 'factors' by asking the students to provide the definitions. Have the students work through Sections A and B on page 11, and Section A on page 12. As they finish each section, go through their answers with them. Look at the information box above Section B on page 12. On the board, complete the factor tree for the number 24. Repeat for numbers such as 30 and 64, ensuring that students recognise that the tree may be started in more than one way. Remind students of the concept of a prime number (a number which only has two factors – 1 and the number itself). Then students can work through Section B on page 12.

Go over the meanings of odd and even numbers as explained in the information box on page 13. Review composite and prime numbers with the students again if you think it is necessary. The exercises on this page ask the students to classify numbers as odd, even, prime or composite. Write a list of numbers on the board and ask students to point out the prime and even, prime and odd, composite and even, and composite and odd numbers. For each set of numbers, ask the student to explain how they arrived at their answers. Students can then complete the exercises on Pupil Book page 13.

CD-Rom activity
■ Whole number concepts

Review the term 'multiples' before the students work through page 14. Go through their answers with them. Have the students do some of the additional activities on multiples. Then have them work through page 15 on number sequences. They can do this in pairs.

Additional activities
Factors and multiples
Introduce sample word problems for factors and multiples like the example given below.
■ A Christmas tree has lights of two different colours that flash at different times. The red lights flash every 3 seconds and the green lights flash every 8 seconds. If the lights are turned on at the same time, after how many seconds will they flash together?

Let the students record when the lights will flash:

RED	GREEN
3 seconds	8 seconds
6 seconds	16 seconds
9 seconds	24 seconds
12 seconds	32 seconds
5 seconds	40 seconds
18 seconds	48 seconds
21 seconds	56 seconds
24 seconds	64 seconds
27 seconds	72 seconds
30 seconds	80 seconds

Look for the seconds that are common to both lights. Relate the problem to the lowest common multiple (LCM).

Additional activities

More factors and multiples

- Jack has 20 sweets and John has 30 sweets. They want to put them in several bags so that they have the same number in each of their bags. What is the largest number of sweets that can be put into each bag?

JACK	JOHN
1	1
2	2
4	3
5	5
10	6
20	10
	15
	30

The largest number that can be used is 10 sweets. Relate the problem to the highest common factor (HCF).

Number sequences

Look at other patterns and sequences besides numbers. For example:

- Complete the sequences.
  a A, F, K, ___, ___, ___.
  b ←, ↑, →, ___, ___, ___.
  c aa, ab, bb, bc, ___, ___, ___.

Chapter 3 Operations on whole numbers

Pupil Book pages 16 to 25

Materials

- counters such as bottle-caps, seeds, marbles, and so on
- $100, $10 and $1 notes (and/or $1 coins)
- 10c and 1c pieces

Objectives

Students should be able to:

 add whole numbers with and without regrouping

 subtract whole numbers with and without regrouping

 multiply whole numbers by one- and two-digit numbers

 divide whole numbers by one- and two-digit numbers.

Suggested approach

Complete the exercises on page 16, using the adding cups as suggested in the additional activities that follow. Let the students complete the exercises on page 17 in either pairs or groups where they can assess and help each other.

Go through the example at the top of page 18, doing additional exercises of the same type. For example:

- Jacob has four 10c pieces and three 1c pieces. He wants to give Sandy 26c. What coins should he change?
- Jacob has five $10 notes and two $1 notes. He wants to put $28 in his piggy bank. How can he do this?

CD-Rom activity
- Whole number operations

The students can work through the exercises in this chapter in order to practise and drill addition, subtraction, multiplication and division. As they work through each section, you may need to review the procedure for each operation.

Additional activities

Adding cups

Make a set of containers that can be used to store objects for counting, such as bottle-caps, seeds, and so on. This may be a series of small boxes or a series of cups in which each compartment represents a place value. It would be useful for the containers to be the same colour as the objects. Using red, green and blue bottle-caps, for example, the rules could be that ten red caps (ones) = one blue cap (a ten); ten blue caps = one green cap (a hundred). No single container or compartment is allowed to hold more than ten items. Some examples are given below.

■ To add 38 and 46, place eight red caps in the red container and three blue caps in the blue container to represent three tens and eight ones. Add six red caps to the red container, but since the total is more than ten (it is 14), ten of the red caps should be exchanged for one blue, adding another blue to the blue container. Then continue by adding the four blue caps. Finally, there should be eight blue caps and four red caps in the containers, representing an answer of 84.

Repeat this procedure for other additions, showing the link between the written problem and the activity. You can also use the adding cups for subtraction.

Multiplication

Make large charts for display in the classroom. These may include: a chart of multiplication tables, a list of the first ten or 20 prime numbers and examples of the commutative law for both addition and multiplication.

Give students questions which can be written more easily and tell them to find a way of rewriting them so that the multiplication is easier.
For example:

22 × 104
20 × 26
10 × 328
50 × 49
10 × 98

In the first example, you could ask students: Do you agree that 104 = 100 + 4? Then 22 × 104 must be the same as 22 × (100 + 4). They can use their calculators to work out the following:

22 × 104
22 × 100   + 22 × 4
2 200   + 88
2 288

They should realise that 22 × 104 is the same as (22 × 100) + (22 × 4).

Calculate: 28 × 98
  98 = 100 − 2
So 28 × 98 must be the same as
28 × (100 − 2).

Use calculators to calculate the following:
  28 × 98
  28 × 100   − 28 × 2
  2 800   − 56
  2 744
28 × 98 is the same as (28 × 100) − (28 × 2).

Give the following additional examples to the students:
■ 28 × 102
■ 45 × 104
■ 12 × 96
■ 15 × 97

Use the exercises on page 26 to assess work covered in the first three chapters. Students should complete the assessment page on their own, and you can check the answers. If necessary, provide additional practice in areas that students are finding difficult.

Chapter 4 Fractions

Pupil Book pages 27 to 29

Materials

- charts showing types of fractions and examples of each
- items that can be divided into fractions, such as oranges, pizza, slices of bread, cakes, sticks of sugar cane, and so on

Objectives

Students should be able to:

- ✓ identify proper and improper fractions and mixed numbers
- ✓ express improper fractions as mixed numbers and vice versa
- ✓ determine and recognise equivalent fractions of a given fraction
- ✓ express fractions in their lowest terms.

Suggested approach

Review the meaning of the terms 'fraction', 'proper fraction', 'improper fraction' and 'mixed numbers'.

The students can work through pages 27 and 28 in order to review work on fractions. Review equivalent fractions and comparison of fractions. Have the students work through the following examples.

CD-Rom activity

- Fractions

- Copy and complete:

$$\frac{1}{2} = \frac{*}{6} \quad = \frac{*}{10} \quad = \frac{*}{18}$$
$$\frac{2}{5} = \frac{*}{10} \quad = \frac{*}{20} \quad = \frac{*}{40}$$
$$\frac{4}{9} = \frac{*}{18} \quad = \frac{20}{*} \quad = \frac{*}{36}$$

Then have the students complete the exercises on page 29.

Additional activities

Make a large fraction chart for the classroom. Use card to make rectangles to show equivalent fractions. For example, use the same basic size rectangle, say 20 cm by 5 cm. Draw rectangles on it of different sizes, divided according to the fractions. The rectangles can be either cut up or placed over each other to show the relationship between different fractional amounts – halves, quarters, and so on.

Chapter 5 Operations with fractions

Pupil Book pages 30 to 36

Materials
- as for Chapter 4

Objectives
Students should be able to:
- ✅ add and subtract fractions with the same denominator
- ✅ add and subtract fractions with different denominators
- ✅ multiply a fraction by a whole number
- ✅ multiply a fraction by a fraction
- ✅ divide a fraction by a whole number and vice versa.

Suggested approach

Most of the material in Chapter 5 has been covered in the earlier levels. The activities largely take the form of practice and drill, so you can have the students work section-by-section through the exercises on pages 30 to 33. Discuss and check their work as they go along. You may want to work through cancelling (page 34) on the board.

Pupil Book page 30 deals with addition and subtraction of fractions with different denominators. Students have already had some experience of finding the LCD. Go through the examples in the information box with the students. Write up a few more examples on the board and work through these with the class. Leave the examples on the board as the students work through the exercises up to page 34.

Turn to page 35. Read through the examples in the information box, and work through some similar examples on the board. The 'talk about' box on page 35 points out that we call a 25c coin a 'quarter'. The students should work out that 25c is one-fourth, or a quarter, of 100c. Students should be able to work section-by-section through the rest of the chapter, as before.

Additional activities

Try to show the use of fractions in as many everyday activities as possible. For example, we use fractions when telling the time, sharing money or food and measuring things. Students can complete the following activities:

1 A slice of pizza costs $6. A large pizza costs $25. A large pizza is divided into six slices.
   a   If six people each want one slice of pizza, would it be more economical for them to buy their pizza by the slice, or to buy a whole pizza? Why?
   b   If two people each want two slices of pizza, would it be more economical for them to buy their pizza by the slice, or to buy a whole pizza? Why?
2 How many quarter litres of milk are needed to fill a 2 litre jug?
3 Record the activities that you complete on a Saturday from the time you wake until you go to bed. Calculate the fraction of the day spent doing activities such as eating, sleeping, studying, helping around the house, watching television, and so on.
4 With an adult, note how long the evening news lasts and the length of each commercial break during the news. Calculate the length of the commercials as a fraction of the length of the news. Repeat for another type of programme, such as a movie.

Chapter 6 Decimals

Pupil Book pages 37 to 41

Materials
- place value charts showing thousands, hundreds, tens, ones, tenths, hundredths and thousandths
- hundred chart

Objectives

Students should be able to:

✓ determine the place value of digits in decimals

✓ compare and order decimals

✓ convert decimals to fractions and vice versa

✓ add and subtract decimals

✓ multiply a decimal by a whole number.

Suggested approach

Draw the following on the chalkboard:

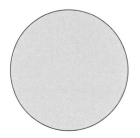 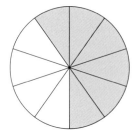

Ask: What fraction is shaded? (1⁶/₁₀.) Have the students write the number in a place value chart, as follows:

ones	tenths
1	6

Now draw the following diagram:

  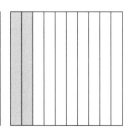

Ask: What fraction is shaded? (2 ²/₁₀.) Have the students write the number in a place value chart again:

ones	tenths
2	2

Give other examples for the students to name the amount shaded and write the fractions in a place value chart. Demonstrate how we can write the fractions without a place value chart (1.6, 2.2, and so on). Explain that these are known as decimals and that the dot is called a decimal point.

Draw a number line like the following on the board:

Show how a number line with decimals can be drawn in the same way.

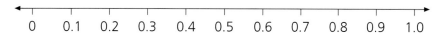

Explain that the sequence of decimals ascends in the same way as whole numbers or decimals. Write some sequences of decimals for the students to continue or fill in the missing numbers.

Let the students work through Sections A and B on Pupil Book page 37.

Display a hundred chart like the one on the left. Point out that the square is divided into one hundred small squares, and that each small square is $\frac{1}{100}$ of the big square. Shade one of the small squares to illustrate this point. Now shade the next column of ten squares, as shown on the left.

Explain that ten squares are equal to $\frac{10}{100}$ or $\frac{1}{10}$. If necessary, revise with students how to simplify fractions.

Show the following on the board:

$\frac{1}{100}$ $\frac{10}{100}$ or $\frac{1}{10}$

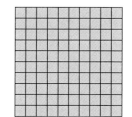 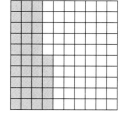

ones	tenths	hundredths
1	3	5

Ask students what fraction of the diagram is shaded ($1\frac{35}{100}$). Have them write the number in a place value chart, as shown on the left.

Now show another diagram:

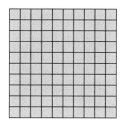 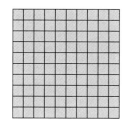 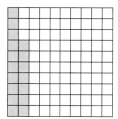

ones	tenths	hundredths
2	1	7

Ask the students what fraction of the diagram is shaded ($2\frac{17}{100}$). Have them write the number in a place value chart, as shown on the left.

Give other examples for the students to name the amount shaded and write the decimals in a place value chart. Do not forget to include examples that will involve zeroes in the tenths place. Demonstrate that, as before, the decimals can be written without a place value chart (1.35, 2.17, and so on). Remind the students that these are known as decimals and that the dot is called a decimal point.

Let the students work through the rest of the exercises on pages 37, 38 and 39.

Turn to page 40. Work through the procedure for converting fractions to decimals and vice versa. Have the students complete some examples on the board. Then they can work through the exercises on pages 40 and 41. Use the exercises on page 42 to assess work covered on fractions and decimals so far.

Chapter 7   Operations with decimals

Pupil Book pages 43 to 51

Objectives

Students should be able to:

 add and subtract decimals

 multiply a decimal by a whole number.

Suggested approach

Turn to Pupil Book page 43. Before you let the students work through the exercises on this page, work through some examples of addition and subtraction with and without regrouping. Include some examples that involve decimals.

Turn to page 44. Read through the example in the information box with the students. They should remember how to add, subtract and multiply decimals in columns, as this material was covered in earlier levels. Students can work through the exercises throughout the rest of this chapter section-by-section, as before.

On Pupil Book page 45, read through the first two exercises with the students to make sure that they all know what each of the questions is asking them to do. Answer any questions that the students may have about interpreting the word problems.

Pupil Book pages 46 to 48 give the students more practice in addition and subtraction of decimals with regrouping. Go through each information box before asking the students to complete the relevant section.

The 'talk about' box on page 49 asks students whether distance is the only consideration people take into account when planning trips. Have a discussion about different routes – for example the difference between walking 1 km downhill or uphill, or driving along very rocky roads.

CD-Rom activity
■ Decimals

Pages 50 and 51 give students practice in multiplying decimals using different methods. Go through the rules and information box before asking students to complete these pages.

Additional activities

Create a chart which has 100 equal divisions to show the connection between fractions and decimals. For example, if half of the chart is shaded, this is equivalent to 50 parts out of 100 or 0.5; $^3/_5$ shaded is 60 out of 100 or 0.6, and so on.

Chapter 8 Percentages

Pupil Book pages 52 to 59

Materials

- magazine and newspaper clippings showing percentages in everyday life
- examples of mark sheets and/or report cards which have percentages
- hundred chart
- chart with diagrams illustrating various percentages
- map showing land use in your country
- food labels listing ingredients

Objectives

Students should be able to:

✓ express percentages as fractions and vice versa

✓ express percentages as decimals and vice versa

✓ determine the percentage of a given quantity

✓ apply knowledge of percentages to solve problems involving profit and loss.

Suggested approach

Show the students magazine or newspaper clippings to highlight how percentages are used in daily lives. Examples of suitable clippings are sale advertisements and labels showing the content of nutrients in foods. Make sure that students realise that a percentage is a kind of fraction. They should realise that 25% means $\frac{25}{100}$, 14% means $\frac{14}{100}$, and so on. Ask if they know how to calculate percentages. Ask questions such as:

- How much is 100% of the class?
- How much is 50% of the class?
- How much is 0% of the class?

Let them work out these percentages, assisting if necessary. Demonstrate how to calculate percentages using real-life examples from the clippings. For example, a supermarket may offer 20% off the normal price of an item. You can ask questions such as:

- If the normal price is $30, what is the sale price?

Demonstrate how to work out the percentage: 20% of $30 = $\frac{20}{100}$ of 30. Remind the students that in mathematics, 'of' means we must use multiplication.

$$\frac{20}{100} = \frac{1}{5}$$
$$\frac{20}{100} \text{ of } 30 = \frac{1}{5} \times \frac{30}{1}$$
$$= \frac{1}{5} \times \frac{30}{1}$$
$$= \frac{6}{1}$$
$$= \$6.$$

The sale price is $30 − $6 = $24.

Give them more examples, such as:

- If the normal price is $120, what is the sale price?
- If the normal price is $800, what is the sale price?

Read through the example on page 52. Together with the class, calculate what percentage of the Earth's surface is land.

Write '8 per cent' on the board. Ask:
- What does '8 per cent' mean? (8 out of 100.)
- How can we write '8 per cent' as a common fraction? ($^8/_{100}$.)
- How do we write it using the % symbol? (8%).
- How many squares in the hundred chart should we shade to represent 8 per cent? (Eight.)

Go through some of the exercises on page 52 with the class, and then let them work through the rest of the exercises, as well as Section A on page 53.

Show the students some examples of real school reports. Discuss the percentages in various subjects and ask which is the highest/lowest percentage. Show students how the percentages were calculated. Then let the students complete Section B on page 53.

Use the hundred chart to show the relationship between fractions and percentages. The students can then work through Section C on page 53 and the assessment exercises on page 54.

Go through the information at the top of page 55 with the students. Demonstrate a few more examples of finding the percentages of amounts or quantities. Here are some examples:
- What is 40% of 500?
- 18% of the people at a concert wore woolly hats. There were 250 people at the concert. How many people wore a woolly hat? How many people did not wear a woolly hat?
- There are 1 500 tickets available for a soccer match. 68% of these are sold before the match, and 11% are sold at the door. How many tickets are sold altogether? How many tickets are not sold?
- What is 98% of 2 500?

Also demonstrate how to increase an amount by a percentage. For example:
- When Lydia bought her school shoes, they cost $35. But when Joan went to the shoe shop two months later, the same shoes cost 12% more. How much did Joan's shoes cost?
- A carpenter has a table marked with a selling price of $800. He puts the price up by 15%. What is the new price?

Then students can work through page 55. The 'talk about' box on page 55 asks students to talk about how land is used in their country. Encourage students to think about the kinds of farming that happens in their country and to look at maps showing land use.

Use labels which show the percentage content in various foods. Compare the fat content of a few different food products (for example a chocolate bar, a tin of beans, a box of cereal). Draw attention to the fact that manufacturers represent the contents of their products in different ways. For example, the ingredients are usually given in a list, but this does not tell us what amounts of each ingredient the product contains. Some manufacturers list the vitamins and minerals in their products in milligrams per 100 grams, while others give the percentage of the recommended daily allowance (RDA). Others may call their products 'low fat' or 'less than 10% fat', but this does not necessarily tell us the actual amounts contained. Make sure that you compare information which is given in the same format, and draw the students' attention to the different ways percentages are used in real life. They can then answer the question posed in the 'talk about' box on page 56. Let students work through the exercises on page 56, which offer more practice in problem solving involving percentages.

Look at advertisements that show how percentages are used to determine discounts, sales tax and sale prices. Make sure that the students understand the terms 'cost price' and 'selling price'. Go through the examples on page 57 in order to review profit and loss in dollars. Students should then work through Sections A and B on page 57.

CD-Rom activity
- Percentages

Move on to profit and loss as a percentage. Go through the example at the top of page 58. Work through Section A on that page together with the class, and then go through the example demonstrating how to work out percentage loss. Students can complete the exercises on page 59 in order to practise and drill what they have learned about profit and loss in this chapter.

Additional activities

1 Get students to calculate their percentages in various subjects at the end of the term/semester.
2 Students can conduct simple research to determine:
   - the percentage of boys or girls in the class or school
   - the percentage of the students who live in a particular parish or city
   - the percentage of students taller than a particular height.

Chapter 9 Money

Pupil Book pages 60 to 64

Materials

- samples of local bills and coins of all denominations and also of coins and bills from other countries
- samples of bills, receipts, cheques, deposit and withdrawal slips, credit cards and automatic banking cards
- advertisements from newspapers and magazines showing items on sale and hire purchase

Objectives

Students should be able to:

- ✓ identify the currencies used in various countries
- ✓ write sums of money in numerals given the words and vice versa
- ✓ find the total of amounts of money expressed as coins, bills and a combination of coins and bills
- ✓ identify and be familiar with some of the transactions completed at a bank – writing deposit and withdrawal slips and cheques
- ✓ calculate the interest gained on savings
- ✓ calculate the interest due on loans
- ✓ calculate cost price, selling price, profit and loss.

Suggested approach

Ensure that the students are familiar with the local bills and coins, identifying the unique features of each. Ask questions such as:

- What is the shape of this bill/coin?
- Is it bigger or smaller than ... (compare other bills/coins)?
- What pictures do you notice on this side? And on the other side?
- Which coins have milled edges?
- Which coins have smooth edges?
- What words/dates are inscribed on the coin/bill?
- What else do you notice?

Also introduce the students to the bills and coins of other countries. Introduce other methods used for payment including bank drafts, cheques and direct debit cards. Then let the students complete Section A on page 60.

Review expressing numbers written as numerals in words before moving on to expressing money given in words as numerals. Using real or imitation coins, ask the students to make up amounts such as $2.00, $1.60, $0.80, and so on. Ask questions such as:

- Which coins would I use to make up an amount of $2.50 using five coins?
- What other combinations of coins could I use to make $2.50?
- What is the biggest number of coins I could use to make $2.50?

The students should recognise that there is more than one way to make up the same sum of money. Then go through the same activity, but ask the students to make up sums of money using as few coins as possible or a given number of coins. The students can then complete page 61, Sections A and B.

Chapter-by-chapter support

Ask who has been to a bank and what they did there. Some students may have their own bank accounts and should be able to suggest some aspects of banking, such as filling in deposit slips and withdrawal slips, using an automated teller machine (ATM), and so on.

The 'talk about' box on page 61 asks students what information is given on a cheque and why this information is important to the bank. The students should realise that the cheque must include the name and account number of the person who is paying the cheque, the name of the person who is receiving the money, the amount – in words and in numerals, the name of the bank, and the date. Show students how to write out a cheque, discussing the advantages and disadvantages of using cheques. Some of the advantages include: cheques allow people to pay large sums of money without withdrawing a lot of cash, which might be easy to lose; cheques can also be made out to one particular person, so that the money can only go into the intended payee's account. However, cheques can also expire if they are not deposited in time (six to twelve months, depending on the bank), and there is also a high incidence of cheque fraud.

Use deposit and withdrawal slips from the bank to show how they are completed. Also show examples of credit cards and automatic banking cards, and discuss how these are used. Include the following points in your discussion:

- the importance of the number and expiry date on a credit card
- the procedure for approving a credit card sale
- the importance of personal identification numbers (PINs) when using automatic banking cards.

Students may find it fun to suggest ways of remembering a PIN and keeping it secret. Also discuss how the bank makes money – by lending money to individuals and businesses, mortgages, bank charges for services and use of machines, and so on. Then the students can complete the exercises on pages 62 and 63. Point out that there are many ways we use money – ask students to suggest ways that we use money every day, for example purchasing food and supplies, payment for services, wages, and so on.

The 'talk about' box at the bottom of page 63 asks students to consider why sellers sometimes sell things at cost price or a loss. Students should realise that sometimes sellers would prefer to recoup some of their expenses immediately rather than wait until they can sell an item for its full price. This is especially true for people who sell perishables, such as fruit and vegetables. They would rather discount the price of the goods while they are still fairly fresh than wait too long and be unable to sell the goods because they are rotten.

Use the money problems on page 64 to give students practice in problem solving involving money.

Additional activities

Have students do some or all of the following activities. In some cases, they will need you to assist them, for example in arranging a guest speaker. You may wish to arrange the visit to a supermarket as a class outing, or let students do this activity as homework.

1 Visit a local shop or supermarket to see how purchases are made and how goods are advertised and promoted.
   a Choose a particular product, for example spaghetti, or soap. Have a discussion about how different companies advertise the same product. How do they persuade people to buy their product?
   b How would you choose the most economical purchases when you go shopping?
   c Why do you think people buy the more expensive products?
   d What do the following terms mean: 'buying in bulk' and 'buying wholesale'?
   e How do retailers make a profit from buying wholesale and selling to customers?
2 Make a coin collection of coins from the Caribbean islands. Try to identify on the map the places where the coins are used.
3 Start a bank for the class, with permission from students' parents and principal. This will help you to learn the value of saving money.
4 Invite a guest speaker to address your class on the functions of the credit unions or cooperative societies. The speaker will be able to explain the advantages and disadvantages of saving using banks versus credit unions or cooperative societies.
5 Identify your favourite TV, magazine or newspaper advertisement and why you like it.
   a Work in groups to create a poster which advertises a product such as school supplies or a computer.
   b Show your posters to the rest of the class and describe your product in a way that will convince your classmates to buy the product.

For the next activity, students work in groups. Give each group an advertisement or flyer from a local restaurant or supermarket. Each group is then given a limited sum of money and asked to make purchases based on a number of criteria, for example:
- Buy ten items that cost less than a total of $25.00.
- Buy items that would make up a meal, including a carbohydrate, a salad and a drink, spending less than $16.00, and so on.

| Chapter 10 | Lines and angles |

Pupil Book pages 65 to 70

Materials
- paper and card for folding
- geometry tools – rulers, protractors, pencils

Objectives
Students should be able to:
- ✓ identify and draw horizontal and vertical line segments
- ✓ identify and draw parallel and perpendicular lines
- ✓ identify right angles
- ✓ describe acute, right, obtuse, straight and reflex angles
- ✓ classify angles as acute, right, obtuse or reflex.

Students dealt with lines and line segments in Level 4. Revise these concepts using the information box at the top of page 65. Then draw a vertical line on the board. Explain that vertical lines are drawn from North (up) to South (down) or from South to North. Now draw a horizontal line on the board and explain that horizontal lines are drawn from East (right) to West (left) or from West to East. Ask volunteers to come to the board and draw horizontal and vertical line segments.

Read through the rest of the information box on page 65. Draw a rectangle on the board and ask a student to draw in the diagonal. Students can then complete the exercises on pages 65 and 66.

Draw a square on the board and ask a student to draw in its diagonals. Ask the student to point out where the two diagonals meet. Explain that we say that the two lines intersect and that we can label the line of intersection with a letter.

Ask another student to draw a vertical line and a horizontal line that intersect each other. Ask the students what angle the two lines make. They should be able to tell you that the lines intersect at right angles. Explain that when two lines intersect each other at right angles, we call the lines perpendicular lines.

Read through the information box to describe parallel lines to the students. Emphasise the fact that parallel lines will never meet, or intersect. They will always be the same distance apart from each other. Ask the students to think of other examples of parallel lines in real life. Students can now complete the exercises on pages 67 and 68.

Introduce angles using page 69. Read through the information about angles, and demonstrate the concept of an angle by folding a piece of paper or card. Have the students make their own right angles out of paper or card. Before you go through Section A with the students, point out some examples of these right angles – the door, the board, the corner of the desk, and so on. You can take the students on a walk around the school to identify other angles in the design of buildings, windows, furniture, decorations, and so on. Then work through Sections A and B on page 69 with the class.

In pairs, the students can read through the information and exercises in Section A on page 70. Ask the students to classify angles seen in the classroom and in the environment. They should be able to identify acute, right, obtuse and reflex angles. Ask volunteers to come to the board and draw examples of each of these types of angles. Then draw your own examples of these angles on the board, and ask volunteers to label each type of angle. Students can then work through Section B.

CD-Rom activity
■ Lines and angles

The 'talk about' box on page 70 asks students what a protractor looks like and how many degrees are in a right angle. If necessary, show students a protractor. Let them describe it carefully and show how to use it to measure the sizes of angles. Students should know that a right angle measures 90 degrees.

Chapter 11 Plane shapes

Pupil Book pages 71 to 81

Materials
- pictures and photos showing angles and polygons
- geometry tools – rulers, protractors, pencils
- chart showing types of angles
- chart showing types of triangles
- chart showing types of quadrilaterals
- chart showing the parts of a circle
- examples of various polygons
- map with coordinates
- grids of squared paper for the students to use
- paper and ink
- mirror

Objectives
Students should be able to:
- ✓ identify right angles
- ✓ describe acute, right, obtuse, straight and reflex angles
- ✓ classify angles as acute, right, obtuse or reflex
- ✓ measure and draw angles
- ✓ identify the number of sides, vertices and angles in a given polygon
- ✓ describe and identify triangles, quadrilaterals and pentagons
- ✓ classify and name equilateral, isosceles, scalene and right-angled triangles
- ✓ classify and name quadrilaterals – rectangles, squares, parallelograms
- ✓ identify and name the parts of a circle – centre, radius, diameter
- ✓ state the relationship between the radius and the diameter
- ✓ identify two-dimensional shapes that have the same size and shape
- ✓ explain the concept of congruent figures
- ✓ use a simple coordinate system
- ✓ identify lines of symmetry.

Suggested approach

Explain what a polygon is to the class. Ask the students to identify polygons in their environment. Show the students polygons that may have been cut from card. Ask questions such as:
- How many sides does it have?
- How many angles does it have?
- What types of angles are they?
- How many corners (vertices) does it have?

Have the students complete the exercises on pages 71 and 72. The 'talk about' box on page 72 asks the students what name can be given to all the shapes shown. They should realise that the shapes can be called polygons.

If a camera is available, the students should be encouraged to take photographs of polygons in their environment, describing each one.

The students can draw diagrams to complete a table, similar to the one below, for polygons with up to ten sides.

Shape	Number of sides	Name
	3	triangle
	4	quadrilateral
	5	pentagon

The students can work in groups to reproduce the table on posters which you can display in the classroom.

Make a chart showing different types of triangles and ask the students to describe the triangles in terms of the lengths of the sides and the angles. Have the students complete the exercises on pages 73 and 74. Ensure that the students understand the relationship between the parallelogram, the rectangle and the square.

Turn to page 75. Have the students look at the pictures in Section A. They can write down their own answers to the question. After a few minutes, let them share their answers with the class. Then let them work through the rest of the exercises on pages 75 and 76.

Draw two triangles on the board. Make sure that their size and shape are exactly the same. Ask the students what they notice about these two triangles. (They are the same shape and size.) Explain that when two shapes are exactly the same shape and size, we say that they are congruent.

Now draw more pairs of triangles on the board. For example, one triangle should be bigger than the other, one triangle should have different angles than the other, and in a congruent pair, draw one triangle that is upside down. In each case, ask the students if the triangles are congruent or not and how they know this.

Draw a circle on the board and ask a volunteer to draw a congruent shape. Repeat with different polygons. Students can now complete the exercises on pages 77 and 78. Suggest that the students draw diagrams of the questions on page 78 to help them solve the problems

---

Draw a coordinate grid like the one in the information box on page 79 and label the vertical axis, horizontal axis and origin. Explain to the students that this is a grid. Ask the students if they know how we could give the exact position of any point on the grid. Explain that we use coordinates to do this. Coordinates are a pair of numbers. The first number tells you the horizontal position of the point, and the second number tells you the vertical position of the point on the grid.
Go through the example on page 79 with the students. Then, write up some more coordinates of your own. Ask students to come to the board and plot these points on the grid. You can then draw points on the grid and ask students to name their coordinates.

The 'talk about' box on page 79 asks how coordinates are used in real life. This is where you can talk about map reading. Show students a map and ask them to locate certain places using coordinates. Students can then complete the exercises on page 80.

Remind students that geometric concepts, such as angles, symmetry and congruency, are often used by people in real life, for example artists, craftspeople and builders. Ask the students if they can think of specific examples where these people might use geometric concepts. For example, builders have to know how to measure angles on an architect's plans and need to know how to make these angles when building the house that the architect has drawn.

Introduce symmetry through the practical activity of making 'ink devils'. Students have done this in Level 4, but it is a fun activity that reinforces the concept of symmetry in a practical way. Fold a sheet of rectangular paper into two equal parts and open again. Spread ink (or paint) on one side of the paper and fold again. Rub the paper together, spreading the ink between the folded sheet. Open the paper again and see the ink devil that is created. Each ink devil is symmetrical about its folded centre. Help students to see which shapes have lines of symmetry by placing a mirror at various points on the object. Have the students complete Section A on page 81. Ask them to identify other symmetrical shapes in the environment. Then they can complete the remainder of page 81.

Additional activities

- Encourage the students to create their own charts showing types of angles, polygons, triangles and quadrilaterals. If the students have access to computers, they can learn how to create polygons in word processing or graphics programs.
- Students can also take photographs of buildings, vehicles, furniture, appliances, and so on, highlighting the shapes present in these objects.
- Students can create pictures using coloured cut-out shapes such as rectangles, squares, circles and other polygons.
- Students can use a variety of shapes to create patterns for fabrics or floor tiles.
- Use a tangram. Scramble the tangram pieces and ask the students to form the square again. The pieces of the tangram can also be rearranged to create other figures and shapes.

Chapter 12 Solid shapes

Pupil Book pages 82 to 86

Materials

- paper and card for folding
- pictures and photos showing solid shapes
- solids such as balls, boxes, cones, spheres, cans, and so on
- charts showing types of solids
- nets of solids – cubes, cuboids, cylinders, square-based pyramids
- geometry tools – rulers, protractors, pencils
- tracing paper

Objectives

Students should be able to:

- ✅ identify and name solids – cubes, cuboids, cylinders, prisms, pyramids, cones, spheres
- ✅ classify solids according to their attributes
- ✅ differentiate between the nets of different solids
- ✅ construct solids from their nets.

Suggested approach

Work through page 82 with the students. Show examples of various solids. Ask the students to bring examples of solids to class. For example, they can bring shoe boxes, cereal boxes and other boxes to show different cuboids. Party hats and ice-cream cones are good examples of cone shapes. Some items are packaged in prism-shaped or pyramidal boxes. In addition to bringing the solids to class, the students may also be asked to list and describe solids found around the home. You may want to set this as a homework activity and the students can share their findings the next day. Then have the students complete the exercises on pages 83 and 84.

The 'talk about' box on page 84 asks students to think about how a craftsperson would have made the ornament. Students should realise that the person would need to have knowledge of angles and nets (as the ornament has been made by folding paper).

CD-Rom activity
- Solid shapes

Provide the students with nets of solids. Point out how the nets relate to the solid in terms of number of faces, shape of the faces and the number of vertices. The students will work in groups to make as many solids as possible. If some students wish to make their own nets, provide paper so that they can do this. Then let the students work through pages 85 and 86.

Additional activities

- Students can use coloured card and nets of solids to make decorations.
- Use the nets of solids to illustrate how it is possible to calculate the area of the faces of solids (surface area).

Assessment

Use the exercises on page 87 in order to assess students' grasp of concepts covered in Chapters 9 to 12.

Chapter 13   Measurement

Pupil Book pages 88 to 103

Materials

- paper and card, scissors
- measuring instruments – scales, ruler, measuring tape, measuring cylinder, thermometer, watches, clocks, and so on
- items that can be used for non-standard measurements such as new pencils, pebbles, strips of card
- jar of sweets for estimating numbers
- geometry tools
- empty containers of various capacities
- squared or graph paper
- items that can be measured – ties, ribbons, strips of paper, vegetables, seeds, liquids, and so on
- thermometers
- drawings of irregular polygons
- drawings of shapes on grid paper

Objectives

Students should be able to:

- ✓ identify methods of measuring using non-standard units
- ✓ identify instruments used to measure length, mass, time, capacity, volume and temperature
- ✓ estimate, measure and record lengths in metric units
- ✓ draw lines of a given length
- ✓ convert between the metric units of length, mass and volume
- ✓ use scales to determine distances
- ✓ estimate, measure and record mass in metric units
- ✓ calculate the volumes of cuboids and cubes
- ✓ perform computations using metric units
- ✓ measure and compare temperatures using the Celsius scale
- ✓ determine the perimeters of regular and irregular shapes
- ✓ find the lengths of sides of a polygon given the perimeter
- ✓ determine the areas of regular and irregular shapes
- ✓ identify appropriate units for the measurement of small and large areas
- ✓ derive the formulae for the areas of rectangles, squares and triangles.

Suggested approach

Introduce the students to non-standard systems of measurement. For example, ask three students to draw outlines of their feet onto card. Cut out the outlines and use these as rulers. Measure the length of the classroom using one of these 'rulers'. Ask: How many 'feet' long is the room? Repeat the exercise with another student's footprint and compare the results. Have the students discuss the advantages and disadvantages of using foot lengths as a measuring unit. Then have the students complete the exercises on page 88.

Discuss the questions asked by the 'talk about' box on page 88. Students should realise that length is usually a horizontal distance, height is usually a vertical distance as it is a measure of how tall something is, and distance is a measurement between two points, i.e. how far apart two or more objects are.

Ask questions such as:
- How many students do you think there are in this school?
- How tall do you think I am?
- How many sweets do you think I have in this jar?

Point out that sometimes, when we want to measure something, we start by making guesses about the measurements. Remind the students that guessing in mathematics is called estimating. Have the students complete the practical activity in Section A on page 89.

Examine the relationship between the various units of length – kilometre, metre, centimetre and millimetre. Ask students which unit of length could be used to measure each of the following:
- length of the playing field
- distance from the school to the nearest shop or supermarket
- length of the room
- thickness of a mathematics exercise book
- length of a student's shoe
- distance from Barbados to St Vincent.

Review the method for converting from one unit of length to another. Ask questions such as: If Mr Rowe is 162 cm tall, and Mr Grant is 1 m 75 cm tall, who is taller? Discuss with the students how the question can be answered: we could convert all the measurements to centimetres or convert all measurements to metres and centimetres. Have the students complete Sections B and C on page 89. Then supervise the students as they work through the exercises on pages 90 and 91.

The 'talk about' box on page 91 invites students to think about units other than decimal units. The students should have heard of inches, feet and miles (imperial units). The 'talk about' box also asks students to think about how drivers know how far they have travelled in a car. The distance travelled by a car is registered on the odometer, which keeps a record of the total distance clocked up by that car, as well as a record of the 'trip' distance since the odometer was reset to zero.

For the next activity, you need a sheet of card at least 1 metre square. Tell the class that you are going to draw a picture of a student. Measure the length of the student's head and draw a head of the same length on the card. Then measure the length from the neck to the waist and attempt to draw this on the card. The card will not be long enough. Ask the students what you can do to get the drawing on the sheet. Lead the students into a discussion on the use of scale drawings.

Turn to page 92. Go through the practical activity in Section A with the class, and read through the information in the box above Section B. Then have the students complete the rest of the exercises on pages 92 to 94.

Introduce non-standard units of mass. For the following activity, you will need 20 small pebbles. These will be used to measure mass. Place an exercise book on one side of an equal arm balance. Place pebbles on the other side until the arms balance. How many 'stones' does the book weigh? Have the students find the mass, in stones, of an eraser, ten pencils, and so on.

Examine the relationship between the kilogram and gram. Ask students which unit of mass could be used to measure each of the following:
■ the total mass of five students
■ the mass of an eraser
■ the mass of ten pencils
■ the mass of an exercise book
■ the mass of 20 textbooks.

Review the conversion from one unit of mass to another. Then have the students work through pages 95 and 96.

Turn to page 97. Work through the information at the top of the page together with the class. Show juice boxes of different sizes. Compare their capacities, asking questions such as:
■ How much juice would this box hold?
■ How many 250 ml boxes are needed to fill a 1 l box?
■ How many 250 ml boxes are needed to fill a 2 l bottle?

You can also use containers of different shapes to discuss principles related to volume and capacity. Ask questions such as:
■ Does a bottle hold more because it is taller or does it hold more because it is fatter?
■ What if the two bottles are the same size, but one is made out of very thick glass and the other is made out of thin glass? Which will hold more?

Have the students complete the exercises on pages 97 and 98. The 'talk about' box on page 98 asks students how they could find out the volume of an irregular solid like a stone or a pebble. The students can work in pairs to brainstorm their responses to this question. Let them give their suggestions. The most commonly used method for finding the volumes of irregular solids is as follows. Use a measuring jug or beaker. Fill it with water and make a note of the volume of water in the jug. Drop the irregular solid into the water. The water level will rise to give a new reading. We can use the difference in the readings to work out the volume of the solid.

Turn to page 99. Work through Section A with the class. The 'talk about' box on page 99 asks the students what the temperature table on that page tells them about the seasons in different countries. Have a discussion about the seasons in different countries. Lead students to realise that countries in the northern hemisphere (such as England and Canada) have winter in January. Countries closer to the equator have warm weather all year round. It may be useful to show students a world globe and to discuss the movement of the Earth around the sun and how this movement determines the seasons.

You may also wish to discuss the following aspects:
- temperatures at different times of the day
- temperatures at which water boils and at which it freezes
- temperatures in different parts of the world at the same time of the year
- temperature of the human body.

Let students work through Section B on page 99 in pairs.

If you have thermometers, ask the students to take the temperature of a number of things, such as their body temperature, the air temperature inside and outside the classroom, the temperature of water from the tap, and the temperature of boiling water. Students should record their measurements in degrees Celsius in a table.

Turn to page 100. Work through the practical activity in Section A with the class. In addition, give students drawings of irregular polygons, and ask them to find the perimeters. Ask students when we would need to work out the perimeters of shapes in real life. Here are some possible examples:
- We need to know the perimeter of a plot when we build houses, dig swimming pools, and so on.
- We need to know the perimeter of a mat or carpet in order to make sure that it fits into a room.
- In arts and crafts, we measure the perimeters of shapes we wish to cut out, so that we know how much material (for example, cloth or card) we need.

There are many more examples that students may think of. Have students work through Sections B and C of page 100. Go through their answers with them.

Work through Section A on page 101 with the students. Make sure that students can distinguish between area and perimeter. List a number of objects on the board, for example, a matchbox, a leaf, a country, a football field, etc. For each object you have listed, ask the students what unit of measurement they would use for measuring these areas. Explain that as well as square centimetres and square metres, the students can also use square millimetres and square kilometres to measure area.

Give them some examples of shapes on grid paper, and have them find the perimeter and the area. Then let them work through the exercises on pages 101 to 103.

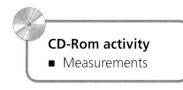

CD-Rom activity
- Measurements

Additional activities

Give students some or all of the following activities.

1 a Research the different units people have used throughout history for measuring distance and length.

b Find out how the following measurements got their names: fathom, pace, hand, yard, chain, cubit, inch, furlong.

c Give the students a list of common objects either in their homes or in the classroom. Ask them the estimate and then measure (you will have to provide the appropriate measuring instruments) the length, mass and/or capacity of these objects. Students can record their measurements in a table.

d Find out why metric and imperial units are used in real life.

2 Research the metric system of measurement. Find out how the base units for length (metre), capacity (litre) and mass (kilogram) were developed.

3 a Draw a plan of the school compound, using an appropriate scale. You can fill in details such as trees and pathways.

b Make a model of the school compound, using cubes, cuboids, cylinders and other solids to represent the buildings and objects.

c Discuss the buildings on the compound with respect to:
- where they are situated in relation to each other
- the shape of the building
- the size of the building.

4 Solve the following problems.

a A square has a side of 6.2 cm. What is its area?

b A rectangle has a width of 8 cm and a length of 33 mm. What is the area of the rectangle in square centimetres?

c A rectangle has a length of 9 cm and a width of 4 cm. What is the width of a square which has the same area?

Chapter 14 Time

Pupil Book pages 104 to 106

Materials
- clock faces with hands that can be removed
- calendars
- digital and analogue clocks and watches, stopwatches

Objectives

Students should be able to:

 express time using the 12-hour and 24-hour clocks

 represent time on an analogue or digital clock

 calculate starting time, elapsed time and finishing time of given events.

Suggested approach

Introduce the concept of time by asking questions such as:
- Why is it important to know the time?
- What instruments do we use to help us tell the time?
- What is the time now?
- What time do you wake up in the morning?
- What time did this lesson start?
- What time is break?
- Is it the same time in all the countries of the world?

- What time does the sun rise?
- When do you eat lunch?

Let the students complete the exercises on page 104. You can use these questions as a review of work they have already done on time. You could also ask the students to represent their answers to Section A on both an analogue and a digital clock face. This will help to reinforce their knowledge.

Tell the students that on Saturday you ate at eight o'clock. Ask which meal they think you ate. If they suggest breakfast, tell them you ate dinner, and vice versa. Remind the class that you can distinguish between times by using am and pm. Introduce the concept of the 24-hour clock and discuss when we use the 24-hour clock. Some examples might include: train timetables, tickets for transport such as aeroplanes, buses, trains, and so on. TV and radio schedules are also given using the 24-hour clock so that people know what time particular programmes are aired. Have the students complete the exercises on page 105.

Identify students who were born in the same month or no more than two months apart. Determine the age differences between these students in terms of months and days. Then let the students work through the exercises on page 106.

Additional activities

A calendar should be displayed in the classroom, on which students can record their birthdays and the dates of the local holidays such as Independence, Christmas and Easter. You can also give students one or more of the activities that follow.

Measuring instruments through history

1 a Do some research to find out how early civilisations told the time.
  b Make some of the instruments that were used by earlier civilisations for telling the time.

Some examples are given here:
- **To make a water clock:** You will need two empty plastic containers, of similar sizes, such as butter or ice-cream containers. Make a small hole in the side of one container, near to the base. Cover the hole with a piece of tape. Place the container above the other container so that water coming from the hole can fall into the second container. Fill the first container with water and remove the tape. You can fill the 'clock' with water and use it to time simple tasks. For example, skip until the water runs out completely or use it to time class quizzes.
- **To make a sundial:** You will need a piece of cardboard, modelling clay and a pencil. Place the pencil upright on the cardboard, using the modelling clay to keep the pencil upright. Place the sundial outdoors on a flat surface. Mark the location of the shadow of the pencil at different times of the day.

Additional activities

Distance and speed

Six students run a specified distance, individually or two at a time, with students assigned to time the runners. Ask the spectators to guess which student they thought was the fastest runner and to rank the students from fastest to slowest. Help the students to calculate the speed of each student. Compare these calculations with the predictions of the class. The exercise may be repeated with each student running a different distance – one runs 50 m, another 60 m, another 75 m, and so on. Students may also walk. Highlight the relationship between distance, time and speed. For example, if the distance is the same and the time is shorter, it means the speed is greater.

Duration

Students can note the time taken between various television programmes. They can also watch a programme on television and note how many minutes were assigned to advertisements during the programme. You may want to have a class discussion about why TV stations show advertisements.

Chapter 15 Data handling

Pupil Book pages 107 to 115

Materials

- examples of statistical graphs from newspapers and magazines
- squared or graph paper
- cut-out bottle shapes made of card
- small boxes of coloured sweets
- geometry tools

Objectives

Students should be able to:

- ✓ collect data using a variety of methods – interview, questionnaire, observation
- ✓ represent data collected using a table, pictograph or bar graph
- ✓ interpret information seen in pictographs, bar graphs and pie charts
- ✓ determine the mean for a set of data
- ✓ determine the mode for a set of data.

Suggested approach

Ask the students how they would find out the following information:

- how many students are wearing black shoes
- the age of students in the class
- the number of cars in the car park
- the number of boys in the class
- the number of primary and secondary schools in the country.

Highlight the fact that information can be obtained in a number of ways:

- by looking around you
- by asking questions
- by getting people to write their ideas or opinions down.

Assign a student the role of a reporter for the local television station. The reporter must conduct an interview to find out how the students travel to school – bus, car, walk or ride. The reporter will present the information to the entire class the next day. Have the students complete the exercises on pages 107, 108 and 109.

Ask each student to state their favourite drink. Attempt to write every response on the board. After a while, ask the students how you could do this more easily and neatly. Try to elicit the answer that we can put the responses in groups. Students should suggest using tables and tally charts, which they have used at earlier levels. Mark the responses in a tally table, with one tally representing one student. Draw a large template for a bar graph, labelling the x-axis 'names of drinks' and the y-axis 'number of students'. Give each student a piece of paper or card, cut in the shape of a bottle, to place in the correct column or row of the bar graph, representing their favourite drink. Point out to the students that they have completed a pictograph. Ask: What would we call this graph if we filled in blocks on a grid to represent each student? (A bar graph.)

Have the students work in pairs through the practical activity in Section A on page 110. Each pair will need a box of coloured sweets. Go around the class making sure that students understand how to construct their graphs.

For exercise 1 in Section B, students will need the attendance figures for their class. You may want to keep a tally on the board for a week, and let them work out the totals themselves, or else simply write up your own records from the last week. Students should be able to work through the exercises on pages 110, 111 and 112 on their own. Go through their answers with them.

Introduce pie charts using the idea of fractions. For example, show the students how we could draw a pie chart for the data that follows.
- Sandra went to the beach for 6 hours on Saturday. Sandra read her book for 1 hour, played volleyball for 3 hours and slept for 2 hours before going back home. What fraction of the time was spent playing volleyball? What fraction was spent sleeping?

Draw a pie chart to show the data. Explain to the students the relationship between the slices of the pie and the time Sandra spent doing the activities. Then have the students work through the exercises on pages 113 and 114.

Introduce the concepts of means, medians and modes. Read through the information at the top of page 115 with the class, and work through a few examples on the board.

Ask the students how they would find out the following:
- the average number of children in a family
- the most common shoe size in the class
- the average height of students in the class
- the average age of students in the class
- the most popular subject (after mathematics) of students in the class.

The students can then complete the exercises on page 115.

Give the students a project in which they consolidate all of their knowledge about data handling. Ask the students to choose one of the questions listed at the beginning of this suggested approach, or students can choose a question of their own. Students have to collect data to answer the question, select the appropriate method/s to represent their data, and then explain their choices. You could select a few students to give a short presentation about their project, describing how they collected their data and why they chose the data representation methods they did.

Additional activities

Students can compile graphs to show things such as:
- preferred flavours of ice-cream amongst students in their year
- favourite cartoon characters or movie stars
- month of birth of students in their class
- favourite subjects of students in their year.

Students can also collect information on the rainfall for a period of one week from the weather reports on television or in the newspaper and illustrate the information on a bar graph. They can analyse the graph to determine which days had the most rainfall and which days had the least rainfall. They can then repeat the exercise for another week and make a comparison. The exercise could be repeated for a week in each month of the year. The students will then be able to predict which month is likely to have the most rainfall and which the least rainfall.

Assessment
Use the exercises on page 116 in order to assess students' grasp of concepts covered in Chapters 13 to 15.

LESSON PLAN OUTLINE

Date: _____   *Time:* _____ *to* _____

Class: _____   *Age range:* _____

Topic: _____

Concepts to be covered: _____

Objectives:

_____

_____

_____

_____

_____

Materials needed:

_____

_____

_____

_____

_____

Set induction:

_____

_____

_____

_____

_____

Learning experiences
Instructional input and modelling:

_____

_____

_____

_____

_____

_____

_____

Check for understanding:

_____
_____
_____
_____
_____

Give independent practice:

_____
_____
_____
_____
_____
_____

Follow-up activity:

_____
_____
_____
_____
_____
_____
_____

Evaluation of lesson:

_____
_____
_____
_____
_____
_____
_____

Signature of teacher:

_____

Level 5 curriculum coverage grid

Pupil Book 5

c = core   n = new objectives for this edition   e = extension

This grid will be updated in the event of future curriculum changes. For more information on the latest grid, please visit www.pearsoncaribbean.com.

Chapter	Objectives	OECS*	Trinidad & Tobago	Bahamas	Barbados	Jamaica
1	read, write and order numbers	c	c	c	c	c
	determine place value of a digit in a given number	c	c	c	c	c
	write numbers using expanded notation	c	c	c	c	c
	round numbers off to the nearest ten, 100 or 1 000	c	c	c	c	c
	read and write Roman numerals	c	c	c	c	c
	express Hindu–Arabic numbers as Roman numerals and vice versa	c	c	c	c	c
2	identify and use the factors of a given number	c	c	c	c	c
	identify and use prime numbers	c	e	c	c	c
	distinguish between prime and composite numbers	c	e	c	c	c
	express a number as a product of its prime factors	c	e	c	c	c
	determine the highest common factor (HCF) of two numbers	c	e	c	c	c
	identify and use the multiples of a given number	c	c	c	c	c
	determine the lowest common multiple (LCM) of two or three numbers	c	c	c	c	c
	classify numbers using several number concepts, e.g. prime and even, prime and odd, composite and odd, etc	c	e	n	n	n
	complete number sequences	c	c	c	c	c
3	add whole numbers with and without regrouping	c	c	c	c	c
	subtract whole numbers with and without regrouping	c	c	c	c	c
	multiply whole numbers by one- and two-digit numbers	c	c	c	c	c
	divide whole numbers by one- and two-digit numbers	c	c	c	c	c
4	identify proper and improper and mixed numbers	c	c	e	c	c
	express improper fractions as mixed numbers and vice versa	c	c	e	c	c
	determine and recognise equivalent fractions of a given fraction	c	c	e	c	c
	express fractions in their lowest terms	c	c	e	c	c
5	add and subtract fractions with the same denominator	c	c	e	c	c
	add and subtract fractions with different denominators	c	c	e	c	c
	multiply a fraction by a whole number	c	c	e	c	c
	multiply a fraction by a fraction	c	c	e	c	c
	divide a fraction by a whole number and vice versa	c	c	e	c	c
6	determine the place value of digits in decimals	c	c	e	c	c
	compare and order decimals	c	c	e	c	c
	convert decimals to fractions and vice versa	c	e	e	c	c
	add and subtract decimals	c	c	e	c	c
	multiply a decimal by a whole number	c	c	e	c	c
7	add and subtract decimals	c	c	n	c	n
	multiply a decimal by a whole number	c	c	n	c	n
8	express percentages as fractions and vice versa	c	c	e	c	e
	express percentages as decimals and vice versa	c	c	e	c	e
	determine the percentage of a given quantity	c	c	e	c	e
	apply knowledge of percentages to solve problems involving profit and loss	c	c	c	c	e
9	identify the currencies used in various countries	c	c	c	c	c
	write sums of money in numerals given the words and vice versa	c	c	c	c	c
	find the total of amounts of money expressed as coins, bills and a combination of coins and bills	c	c	c	c	c
	identify and be familiar with some of the transactions completed at a bank – writing deposit and withdrawal slips and cheques	c	c	c	c	c
	calculate the interest gained on savings	c	c	c	c	c
	calculate the interest due on loans	c	c	c	c	c
	calculate cost price, selling price, profit and loss	c	c	c	c	c
10	identify and draw horizontal and vertical line segments	c	e	n	c	n
	identify and draw parallel and perpendicular lines	c	e	n	c	n
	identify right angles	c	c	c	c	c
	describe acute, right, obtuse, straight and reflex angles	c	c	c	c	c
	classify angles as acute, right, obtuse or reflex	c	c	c	c	c

*OECS includes Anguilla, Antigua & Barbuda, British Virgin Islands, Dominica, Grenada, Montserrat, St Kitts & Nevis, St Lucia, St Vincent & the Grenadines

Chapter	Objectives	OECS*	Trinidad & Tobago	Bahamas	Barbados	Jamaica
11	identify right angles	c	c	c	c	c
	describe acute, right, obtuse, straight and reflex angles	c	c	c	c	c
	classify angles as acute, right, obtuse or reflex	c	c	c	c	c
	measure and draw angles	c	c	c	c	c
	identify the number of sides, vertices and angles in a given polygon	c	c	c	c	c
	describe and identify triangles, quadrilaterals and pentagons	c	c	c	c	c
	classify and name equilateral, isosceles, scalene and right-angled triangles	c	c	c	c	c
	classify and name quadrilaterals – rectangles, squares, parallelograms	c	e	c	c	c
	identify and name the parts of a circle – centre, radius, diameter	c	e	e	c	c
	state the relationship between the radius and the diameter	c	e	e	c	c
	identify lines of symmetry	c	c	c	c	e
	identify two-dimensional shapes that have the same size and shape	c	e	n	c	n
	explain the concept of congruent figures	c	e	n	n	n
	use a simple coordinate system	c	e	n	n	n
12	identify and name solids – cubes, cuboids, cylinders, prisms, pyramids, cones, spheres	c	c	c	c	e
	classify solids according to their attributes	c	e	c	c	e
	differentiate between the nets of different solids	c	c	c	c	e
	construct solids from their nets	c	c	c	c	e
13	identify methods of measuring using non-standard units	c	e	c	c	e
	identify instruments used to measure length, mass, time, capacity, volume and temperature	c	c	c	c	c
	estimate, measure and record lengths in metric units	c	c	c	c	c
	draw lines of a given length	c	c	c	c	c
	convert between the metric units of length, mass and volume	c	e	c	c	c
	use scales to determine distances	c	e	c	c	e
	estimate, measure and record mass in metric units	c	c	c	c	c
	calculate the volumes of cuboids and cubes	c	c	c	c	c
	perform computations using metric units	c	c	c	c	c
	measure and compare temperatures using the Celsius scale	c	e	c	c	c
	determine the perimeters of regular and irregular shapes	c	e	e	c	c
	find the lengths of sides of a polygon given the perimeter	c	e	e	c	c
	determine the areas of regular and irregular shapes	c	c	c	c	c
	identify appropriate units for the measurement of small and large areas	c	c	n	c	n
	derive the formulae for the areas of rectangles, squares and triangles	c	c	e	c	c
14	express time using the 12-hour and 24-hour clocks	c	c	c	c	e
	represent time on an analog or digital clock	c	c	n	c	n
	calculate starting time, elapsed time and finishing time of given events	c	e	c	c	c
15	collect data using a variety of methods – interview, questionnaire, bservation	c	c	c	c	c
	represent data collected using a table, pictograph or bar graph	c	c	c	c	c
	interpret information in pictographs and bar graphs	c	c	c	c	c
	interpret information in pie charts	e	c	c	c	c
	determine the mean for a set of data	c	c	c	c	c
	determine the mode for a set of data	c	c	c	c	c

*OECS includes Anguilla, Antigua & Barbuda, British Virgin Islands, Dominica, Grenada, Montserrat, St Kitts & Nevis, St Lucia, St Vincent & the Grenadines